THE CHRISTIAN AND JURY DUTY

PEACE·AND·JUSTICE·SERIES 14

THE CHRISTIAN AND JURY DUTY

DUANE RUTH-HEFFELBOWER

Herald Press
Scottdale, Pennsylvania
Waterloo, Ontario

Library of Congress Cataloging-in-Publication Data
Ruth-Heffelbower, Duane, 1949-
The Christian and jury duty / Duane Ruth-Heffelbower.
p. cm. — (Peace and justice series ; 14)
Includes bibliographical references.
ISBN 0-8361-3562-8 (alk. paper)
1.Jury—United States—Miscellanea. 2. Jury—Religious aspects—Christianity. I. Title. II. Series.
KF8972.Z9R87 1991
347.73'0752—dc20
[347.307752] 91-13624
CIP

The paper used in this publication is recycled and meets the minimum requirements of American National Standard for Information Sciences—Permanence of Paper for Printed Library Materials, ANSI Z39.48-1984.

THE CHRISTIAN AND JURY DUTY

Library of Congress Catalog Number: 91-13624
International Standard Book Number: 0-8361-3562-8
Printed in the United States of America
Cover and book design by Gwen M. Stamm

1 2 3 4 5 6 7 8 9 10 97 96 95 94 93 92 91

To all those working
for restorative justice.

Contents

Preface

To serve or not to serve on a jury?

This question is a relatively recent one for Mennonites and members of such historic peace churches as Church of the Brethren and Brethren in Christ. (Although committed to peace, the Quakers, or Society of Friends, have been less troubled by jury duty or participation in government.)

This book was originally commissioned by Mennonite Central Committee because Mennonites needed to examine the issues. It is written from an Anabaptist/Mennonite perspective.

However, the book hopefully will serve all who value the heritage of the sixteenth-century Anabaptists. It can benefit any Christian who wants to examine how faithfulness to God and jury service fit together. It is intended to be relevant in both Canada and the United States.

Before the 1960s, Mennonites were seldom called for jury service, and some conference resolutions and confessions specifically rejected jury service for Mennonites. Then as Mennonites moved off the farm and began to participate in city life, their names wound up on jury lists more frequently.

Mennonites have historically avoided participation in government in general and the court system in particular. Thus jury service has raised serious questions for the many now called.

Can people who practice nonresistant love toward enemies participate in a system which relies on the threat of violence to enforce its judgments? Can people who would forgive one who robbed them be party to imprisoning a person who robbed someone else?

These questions trouble many today. With the number of jury trials steadily increasing, calls for jurors become more frequent. Does jury service violate biblical teaching? Is it proper for a follower of Jesus Christ to serve on a jury? How can we examine the issues and decide what to do?

This book is not an attempt to give the "right" answers to these complex question. Rather, its purpose is to present the options in order to help believers decide for themselves, through the power of the Holy Spirit, what faithfulness to God requires of them.

This book was originally published as *The Christian and Jury Duty* by Mennonite Central Committee. This edition has been completely revised and expanded. Special thanks are due to Keith Regehr who prepared the initial research draft, as well as to Ruby Friesen Zehr for her editorial work on the first edition. Thanks also to the many people in both Canada and the United States who read drafts and offered comments.

—Duane Ruth-Heffelbower
Fresno, California

CHAPTER 1

An Overview of the Legal System

Some Background

Why are there juries? Where did the jury system come from? Is a jury trial really the best way to make a decision?

What is a court?

No matter how complicated they may seem, no matter whether they are civil or criminal, modern court cases are nothing more than disputes between people.

Every group of people must have some method for handling disputes. In an earlier day, dispute methods were informal. But as society became more complex, formal methods replaced informal ones. Written laws replaced informal customs. Courts replaced the marketplace or the city gate as places to settle disputes. A court is nothing more than a person, or several people, who judge people's disputes. That much hasn't changed for thousands of years.

While some type of courts have existed for thousands of years, informal methods of settling disputes were most common until modern times. As nations developed, governments created courts and laws which eventually had the right to settle both criminal and some civil disputes. (We will see later the difference between civil and criminal.)

In addition, these courts were available for other cases which citizens chose to bring to them. Most disputes are still handled informally, but the court system gets a much larger share of them than in earlier times.

Canadian and United States court systems

The legal systems of Canada and the United States both developed from the English legal system, which in turn developed from a complex set of roots. These included tribal practices of the Angles and Saxons, traditions of the Norman conquerors, the Bible, and perhaps various influences from the rest of Europe and even Asia.

Although details of the legal systems of Canada and the United States differ, they are basically similar. Both systems provide courts where people represented by lawyers can bring their cases for a decision. Both provide the possibility of having the decision made by a jury of citizens.

In both countries, a jury is used only when the people involved request it. As a result, many cases are decided by a judge alone. It is also possible in both countries for individuals to present cases without lawyers to help or represent them.

In this book we will concern ourselves only with cases in which a jury has been requested. Since it is rare for people to represent themselves in a jury trial, we will also assume the involvement of lawyers. Representing yourself in a jury trial is usually just a slow way to plead guilty.

Why have juries?

The question remains—why have juries at all?

Juries as we know them began relatively late in history, during the fifteenth and sixteenth centuries. Before then, trials were generally decided by witnesses, by ordeal, by oath, by inquest, and by battle—depending on the nature of the case and the choice of the parties. (The word *party* is used instead of *person* because one of the parties may be a corporation, partnership, government, or some other group instead of a single person.)

Trial by witnesses involved swearing by official witnesses to the facts of the case. In trial by oath, the parties to the case swore to the facts. They were backed up by witnesses who would swear to their honesty.

One form of trial by ordeal required the accused person to be tied up and thrown into water blessed by a priest. It was thought that an innocent person sank, whereas a guilty person was expelled by the holy water and floated. Drowning in a trial by ordeal proved your innocence and at least protected your family against losing all its property, since it was common practice for the king to claim a condemned person's property.

In a trial by inquest, the people from the community were asked to gather and advise the investigating official of the facts in a case. They functioned like a jury, except the jurors were also the witnesses.

Trial by battle called on the parties to a dispute, or their personal champions, to prove or disprove their claim by the outcome of a battle. God's aid was invoked by a priest; it was believed God would assure a just result.

The main functions of the courts in these early trials were to determine the method of trial and to supervise the process.

In A.D. 1215 the church ordered priests not to participate in trials by battle and ordeal. Since priests were needed to bless the trial and invoke God's power, these trial methods were no longer used. The courts then turned to inquest, trial by witnesses, and trial by oath.

By the fifteenth century these methods had developed into a jury system much like ours. It was not until the seventeenth century, however, that judges were forbidden to imprison a jury for giving a decision the judge did not approve.

In the trial of William Penn, the founder of Pennsylvania, the jury was imprisoned five times for refusing to give the verdict wanted by the judge. One juror finally asked a higher court to release him. This court established the important principle that a jury can decide the case contrary to the law, the facts, and the judge.

The ability of the jury to decide a case contrary to the facts and the law is an important principle and a key argument in favor of juries. This ability was one of the jury's most attractive features for the creators of the U.S. system of government.

Feeling that they had suffered under the oppressive yoke of an uncaring and distant king, the people who wrote the U.S. Constitution made the right to trial by a jury of one's peers a fundamental right. No distant ruler could control the outcome of a trial when it was decided by free, local people who had the power to ignore the law and to make a decision without explaining their reasons. Juries were seen as a safeguard of liberty.

The situation in Canada was somewhat different. Here the king was seen as a friendly protector. Canadians never developed the dislike of a justice system imposed by the king found in the United States. For this reason juries were much slower to develop in Canada and the right to a jury trial remains more limited.

Limiting the jury's role

The general movement in courts today is to limit the role of juries and their ability to ignore the law and the facts. Instead of asking for simple yes or no decisions, it is common to ask a jury to make a series of smaller decisions. These decisions then determine the final verdict in ways the jury may not be able to predict. As cases have become more complex, juries have a job which is often too much to ask of untrained people.

Juries are told to decide cases based only on the

facts presented and the law as explained by the judge. Although juries are free to make their own decisions, the risk of having their decisions overturned for failure to follow the facts and the law is greater than ever.

Are juries a safeguard of liberty?

People like Mennonites have historically found themselves at odds with government over such issues as military draft, payment of taxes for war purposes, compulsory public schooling, and Social Security. They have had many occasions to be grateful that juries are free to ignore the law and find people of conscience innocent even when the law has obviously been broken.

Are juries a safeguard of liberty or a way for the majority to oppress the minority? Should there be more or less control of the jury's power? These are old questions still debated today.

Civil and criminal cases

Legal cases are separated into two types: civil and criminal. They are treated differently by courts and the role of the jury is different in each.

Civil cases

Civil cases are suits brought by one person against another. Although the "person" may be a government agency, corporation, or a group of people, it is still considered to be a civil case. Civil cases ask a court to decide things such as whether money is owed, whether a person should be allowed to do something, who owns property, who is at fault, whether a marriage should end, who should have custody of children, and so on.

Criminal cases

Criminal cases are between the government and the people it accuses of committing crimes. National, state, provincial, and some local governments employ a prosecuting attorney. This prosecutor, who determines who will be charged with a crime, is usually called a *district attorney* in the U.S. or a *crown attorney* in Canada. Which prosecutor handles a particular case depends on where the crime occurred and the nature of the crime.

After the prosecuting attorney charges individuals with a crime, the appropriate court orders them to come to court to answer the charge. If they agree that they committed the crime and plead guilty, the judge imposes a punishment, usually a fine or a jail term. If they plead "not guilty," their innocence or guilt is decided at a trial.

Who is entitled to a jury trial?

In a criminal case the accused person may decide whether or not to request a jury trial, although the crime charged must be serious enough to warrant a jury. The degree of seriousness required to allow a jury is greater in Canada than in the United States.

If the jury determines that the person is guilty, the judge passes sentence on that person. Sometimes juries are asked to give sentencing recommendations, including whether or not to impose the death penalty.

In a civil case, either party may request a jury, depending on the nature of the case and the amount at stake. The rules vary. Some cases, such as child custody, are always decided by a judge alone. Other cases may be decided in part by a jury and in part by a judge. Still others are decided by jury alone. The role of the jury in civil cases is to decide who owes what to whom and not to determine guilt as in criminal cases.

Juries have a limited role

Juries have a limited role in both criminal and civil cases. The judge decides which laws apply to the case and orders the jury to consider only those laws, without considering whether the laws are good or not. The judge also decides what the jury can hear and see as evidence, including which witnesses are allowed to speak. The judge can even order witnesses not to give certain testimony.

It is in this context that the jury is asked to decide what happened, who did what, and whether the actions violate the law as described by the judge. If the jury appears to violate the judge's order, the judge can throw out their verdict and grant a new trial.

The jury is not allowed to do any investigation on its own. For example, it may not visit the scene of the crime unless the entire trial is moved to the scene.

The jury is not allowed to watch television, read newspapers, or see anything else pertaining to the case. Jury members may not discuss the case with anyone, including other jurors, until the case is completed. When a case is so notorious that the jury members could not help but hear about it if they went home, the judge can order them kept in isolation until the trial is over.

A jury is not told what the sentence will be if it delivers a guilty verdict in a criminal case. It is usually told almost nothing about the people involved except in unusual cases. The jury may not ask questions of the witnesses, or even suggest questions it would like to have answered (in most cases).

In civil cases the existence of insurance which will pay any award the jury makes is kept secret. The spectacle of someone demanding huge sums of money from a person who obviously doesn't have it is both common and never explained to the jury.

Trials vary greatly in length. Most do not take more than three days, although rare cases may take over a year. Trials in Canada are usually shorter than trials in the United States.

The Adversary System

Fighting it out in court

The legal systems of the United States and Canada are based on an *adversary* system. The parties to the case are seen as competitors who compete with each other to see who will win. The system is based on the belief that truth is best found through open competition; it is the offspring of the twelfth century English trials by ordeal and by battle.

The common phrase "fight it out in court" is a good description of what is happening in modern courtrooms. It is not socially acceptable to settle disagreements by violence. Instead, society has created an orderly system aimed at obtaining a fair settlement without physical violence. Cases are fought out in court instead of under the trees.

It is, however, incorrect to assume that court battles

are not violent. Violence, according to our definition, is the use or threat of deadly force, whether or not it results in death. No matter how complex and sophisticated the legal system appears to be, what it boils down to is two or more people doing battle, in a usually polite way.

The use of a lawyer is very much like the old system of hiring a champion to fight your battle, or in larger cases, of having a private army. This basic concept cannot be overemphasized. A trial is a battle. Life, liberty, and property are as much at stake in a trial as they ever were in battle. The state has approved this form of battle, and the full power of the state, including police and military power, is available to enforce the court's orders.

Judges have the power of the state behind them

During the 1960s, under the order of a U.S. Federal Court, the Army guarded black children entering white schools. The military is used to enforce orders in the case of strikes and large disturbances. Police seize a person's property and sell it when another person has successfully sued him or her. Police seize a person's paycheck for the same reason.

A court can only enforce its orders by the threat, or actual use, of the violent power of the state. When people willingly submit to a court's order, the fact remains that they are submitting under the threat of violence against themselves or seizure of their property.

The trial process makes more sense when seen as a battle. Much of the legal language has military overtones. A lawyer first develops the trial "strategy," after which "tactics" are considered. The truthfulness of witnesses is "attacked" on cross-examination to "destroy" their effectiveness. The prosecuting attorney must "overcome" the presumption of innocence which says that people are considered innocent until they are proven to be guilty.

The violence of the court system

We have seen how our courts enforce their orders by the threat of violence. Does such a system create a violent atmosphere or does it reduce violence?

The current majority view in Canada and the United States is that the legal system reduces violence and protects peaceful people from violent people. It is assumed that a violent person is best prevented from being violent by the threat of violence in return, and that the threat of swift and sure punishment will avoid the need for actual violence in enforcing the law.

To what extent must any society rely on the threat of violence to protect its citizens?

Is it possible for us to live under a government that protects us with the threat of violence without ever being partly responsible for the violence?

Does the legal system provide the best way to settle disputes with a minimum of violence?

How does the Christian's participation in a jury affect the jury system?

What do we owe our society when it comes to participation in the legal system?

Can we in good conscience sit on juries? Can we in good conscience not sit on juries?

The purpose of the rest of this book is to help you consider these questions.

CHAPTER 2
How Juries Work

Jury Selection

You have just received a notice to report for jury duty. How were you chosen? Must you go? What happens next?

How did they get my name?

The answer to this question depends on where you live. In 1961 the U.S. Justice Department reported that each of the ninety-two federal trial courts in the U.S. used a different method of selecting jurors. State, provincial, and local courts also use varying methods.

But all jurors are chosen from lists, usually obtained from government agencies, such as a census bureau, drivers license bureau, voter registration office, or property tax authorities. Some courts have been challenged for choosing jurors from too small a list. A jury chosen from a list of landowners, for instance, would exclude many people, especially the poor.

As governments develop more computer-assisted lists of names, more people find themselves on jury lists. In the past, Mennonites were often not on jury lists because they chose not to vote. Since most of us today own property and drive cars, our names do appear on jury lists.

Must you serve?

Whether you must serve depends on many things. Every court has certain categories of people automatically exempted from jury service. When such people receive their notice, they usually have the option of responding with a note explaining that they fall into one of these categories.

Parents of small children, medical workers, lawyers and their employees, members of the military, police officers, people previously convicted of serious crimes, mentally or physically incapable people, and public officials are exempted by some courts.

Others may be exempted from service if it would cause hardship to them or some other person. They may apply to be excused before they are scheduled to appear in court. People who are self-employed are often excused in the same way.

Exemptions from jury duty

Jury exemptions are constantly changing and judges can excuse any juror. The trend is away from exemptions. California, for instance, does not excuse people because they are blind or deaf. Your local jury official can tell you what rules apply in your area.

Failure to report for jury duty is a crime, and you can be fined or go to jail. When you are called and not excused in advance, you must report or risk being arrested for disobeying the court.

Jury service has financial effects too, since jurors are paid little, if at all. Some employers give jurors time off with pay; others do not. Some employers fire people called to lengthy jury service; in some places laws protect jurors' jobs. Financial hardship alone can allow exemption, although you may need to come to court for questioning by the judge.

Who serves on a jury?

Will you actually serve on a jury if called? That depends. More jurors are called for service than the court expects to use. Jurors are usually asked to wait at the courthouse until the courts needing jurors for that day have selected their juries. Those not selected may then leave. Some courts allow jurors to wait at home or at work until called. Courts vary on the number of days a person must be available for jury service.

Jury selection is a process of elimination that involves questioning of potential jurors. When the court is ready to begin this selection process, it brings in a larger group of potential jurors than needed. The judge explains briefly what the case is about, identifies the parties to the case, and asks questions of the entire group. Jurors may also be questioned one by one.

Courts vary in how jurors are questioned. Some

judges prefer to do all the questioning themselves; others allow lawyers to do most of the questioning. The judge decides how it will be done.

Jurors lose some of their privacy

All the parties to the case will have a list of the jurors' names and addresses. They will probably also have copies of questionnaires filled out by the jurors.

In important cases lawyers will often hire a private investigator to make a report on each potential juror. Sometimes lawyers hire a psychologist to recommend the kind of people to look for in the jury. On the basis of the investigator's report, they identify which jurors on the list are most likely to support the lawyer's case.

Jury reporting services also prepare reports on all potential jurors in the hope of selling them to the parties involved in the case. In many cases there will have been a brief investigation of your voting registration, residence, and work. A potential juror is not a private person.

Many courts allow free questioning of potential jurors. The type of case will influence the questions. If the accused person is a member of a racial minority group, you will be probed for prejudice. If the case involves an automobile accident, your attitudes and experience regarding driving and responsibility for accidents will be interesting to the questioners. If alcohol was involved, your feelings about drinking will be important.

The purpose of this questioning is to test your attitudes on specific issues as well as to get an impression of you as a person, since your role may be decisive in the outcome of the case. Questioning by lawyers has the added purpose of trying to engage your sympathies on their side of the case. For this reason lawyers are nice to jurors unless, for some reason, they suspect that you are prejudiced against their case. Then they may try to provoke you into exposing your prejudice.

Raising personal objections to jury service

Many judges will give an opportunity early in the process for people to raise their personal objections to jury service. When this is not the case, people who feel they cannot participate in the jury for religious or other reasons should raise this concern during the individual questioning. At this point, a lawyer who believes that you cannot give a fair, unbiased decision may ask the judge to excuse you "for cause."

The decision of whether or not to excuse you, whatever the reason, is made by the judge, who may want to question you further before making that decision. If you are objecting to service on religious grounds, the judge may or may not question you sharply. (See Elsie Epp's story in Appendix A.) Many judges are devoutly religious themselves and are convinced that there is no proper objection to jury service on religious grounds.

Judges do not want to excuse jurors unless they are satisfied they should be excused to prevent injustice. To excuse jurors too easily is seen as being unfair to those who do serve.

Lawyers work hard to select a jury which is at least impartial. At the same time judges guard against shopping for sympathetic jurors. At some point before you are accepted as a juror, you will be asked whether there is any reason why you feel you cannot give an impartial decision in the case.

Swearing in the jury

Potential jurors are asked to swear to the truth of their answers before the questioning starts. Their answers are recorded in a transcript along with all other testimony. Testimony by jury members is taken seriously—sometimes cases have been reversed after they were completed when it was discovered that a juror lied during questioning on some significant point.

Asking to be excused from jury service

If you feel that you cannot serve on a jury, you need to be careful how you inform the court. If, for instance, you believe you cannot serve for religious reasons, it is best to say just that, without details. This allows the judge to decide how far to go into the specifics. Many judges will excuse you immediately rather than risk some sort of theological discussion. Others will question you at length, perhaps to make an example of you in some way.

It is a mistake to begin your request for exemption with a judgmental statement, such as, "I don't believe it is possible for any Christian to be a juror." Such blanket statements based on personal conviction may prejudice a whole group of jurors, raising the possibility of the judge having to release them all.

The same thing happens when potential jurors say they know that police officers or people accused of crime can't be trusted. A judge may respond in anger to such statements and may even hold the offending juror in contempt of court, raising the possibility of jail or a fine.

Excusing jurors

When no more jurors are eligible to be excused by the judge for cause, the lawyers take turns excusing a certain number of jurors for no stated reason. These are called "peremptory challenges." The number of these varies depending on the court, the type of case, and the number of parties. Whenever a person is excused, a new potential juror is called forward and questioned as the first group was.

Through peremptory challenges lawyers can keep certain types of people off a jury. Some people feel that there should be a limitation on the use of peremptory challenges. The U.S. Supreme Court has ruled that the systematic removal of racial minorities from juries is unconstitutional. However, since lawyers are not required to state the reason for excusing a juror by this method, it is difficult to prove improper discrimination.

When all peremptory challenges have been utilized, or when all lawyers are satisfied with the jury, the jury is complete. It is asked to swear that it will decide the case properly, according to the evidence and the judge's instructions.

The jury's duty

The jury's job is to listen to the opposing cases presented, look at physical evidence, and decide, based on the evidence and the judge's instructions, what the facts of the case are. When one person claims money from another person, one "fact" of the case is how much, if anything, is owed. In a criminal case the jury decides the "fact" of guilt or innocence of the crime charged. The jury may also be asked to advise the judge on sentencing in certain cases, although in most cases the jury will have no say in the sentence.

What a jury sees

Cases are presented in different ways to judges and juries. Jury trials take two or three times as long as trials by a judge alone. One reason for this is that jurors are not thought able to weigh certain types of evidence properly, thus extreme care is taken to keep the jury from being "prejudiced" by hearing such evidence.

A common example is the use of *inflammatory evidence.* Photographs of the broken bodies of accident victims are considered inflammatory. The question is whether the information jurors might gain from the pictures is more important than the harm done by exposing them to images which might inflame passion or prejudice.

Another example of evidence kept from the jury is *hearsay*. The statement, "He said the light was green," is hearsay because it is secondhand. There are many rules regarding the use of this kind of evidence. A judge hearing a case without a jury would want to hear such evidence and then decide whether or not to give weight to it, but jurors are usually not believed capable of such discretion.

All of this means that the picture of a case as presented to a jury is less complete than a picture of the same case presented to a judge. There are frequent interruptions while lawyers and judge decide whether or not evidence may be presented to the jury. Thus the trial moves slowly and the jury has to fit the pieces of the case together. Since the jury must decide the case only on the evidence presented, great care is taken to include even the most minute details, assuming they are permissible for a jury to hear.

Witnesses

Jurors receive *evidence* from *witnesses*. Some witnesses actually saw what happened and can describe it. Others are expert witnesses who are able to explain how something works. Still other witnesses may have been in charge of part of the investigation and can report on that.

Documents are presented by the witnesses who created them, received them, saw them, found them, or had control of them. Even objects are presented by witnesses who are knowledgeable about them. Each witness is presented by one party after which the other parties may cross-examine that witness.

Cross-examination is an attempt to determine whether witnesses are telling the truth, whether they really saw what they think they saw, whether they really know what they say they know. It is also intended to help the jury decide whether the evidence presented by the witnesses really supports the case of the party that called them.

Cross-examination is one of the keys to the adversary system. First one party presents its case through witnesses who are attacked by cross-examination, then the other side does the same. The assumption in this battle is that the jurors will sift the truth out of the mass of competing claims and that justice will prevail.

The judge instructs the jury

After the total case has been presented, the judge again instructs the jury. Some of the instructions are on how to go about deciding the case. Most of the instructions, however, are about the law which applies to the case as decided by the judge.

Instructions are carefully written, since a higher court will reverse a decision if it determines that an instruction may have misled the jury. The jury is also given instructions that have been written by the lawyers presenting the case and accepted by the judge after a process of argument among the lawyers.

Jury instructions are critical to a case. They tell the jurors what they must decide if they find certain things to be true. It is common for a judge to read instructions to the jury for over an hour.

Instructions are so carefully crafted that many judges will refuse any requests for further explanation. A puzzling instruction may be reread as often as the jury likes. Then the jury will be instructed to decide the case based only on the evidence presented, the law given to them in the instructions, and their common sense.

How the jury decides the case

After the jury has been instructed, it is locked in a room to decide the case. A court official, usually called a bailiff, provides for the jury's needs, taking them out to eat meals as a group or having food brought in. The jury is not allowed to discuss the case with anyone else.

If the jurors have a question, they must tell the bailiff who tells the judge. All the parties and lawyers reassemble in the courtroom to hear the jury's question, which becomes a part of the record of the trial. The judge will usually confer with the lawyers before answering the question.

The judge will not give any interpretation of the evidence and, usually, no further interpretation of the law. However, the jury may hear testimony read from the trial transcript or see physical evidence again. Then it is told, politely, to decide the case by itself.

A jury is not supervised. How and on what basis it decides the case is known only to the members of the jury. When the jury has a verdict everyone reassembles to hear it. At this point jurors may be asked individually if they agree with the verdict. The jury is then excused.

When a jury cannot reach a verdict the judge will prod the jurors to do so, reminding them that it is their duty and that if they cannot decide the trial will have to be repeated. Some judges have been heavy-handed in cases like this. Cases have been overturned on appeal to a higher court because a judge too harshly demanded that unwilling jurors agree to a verdict.

How jurors behave when they are deliberating has been the subject of books, plays, and motion pictures. Their secret exercise of power is fascinating. Sometimes the judge will require the jury to make a series of decisions in which each individual decision sets up different options for the decisions that follow.

But a jury does not have to say how a decision was reached. And it is free to do as it likes. A jury is told to decide on the basis of evidence, but there is nothing to keep it from deciding on the basis of racial prejudice. This can happen unconsciously as jurors decide which witnesses to believe. Jurors generally tend to believe some witnesses, such as police officers, rather than others, such as heroin addicts.

Juries can ignore the law

A jury can find a person guilty of a lesser offense than charged, such as trespassing instead of burglary. Or it can find that the person suing for money wins but is awarded very little money. A jury can decide that the rich company should pay the poor person money even though the evidence shows the company owes nothing.

This ability of the jury is what makes it both popular and unpopular. Some feel that juries protect citizens from a harsh and uncaring government. Others feel that juries allow popular passions and prejudice to overcome the rule of law.

If after much deliberation the jury cannot agree on a verdict, it is called a *hung* jury. The jury is dismissed and the parties will have to decide whether to request a new trial or to resolve the dispute by a settlement.

Jurors are sometimes interviewed by parties to get an idea of how they saw the case. Although jurors do not have to discuss the case with anyone, their impressions can sometimes help settlement talks.

After the trial

The option of whether or not to appeal a case remains even when the jury has reached a verdict. Jurors may again be interviewed to help a party decide whether or not to appeal, or whether to offer a settlement to avoid an appeal. Again, the jurors are not required to discuss the case.

Jury misconduct

Sometimes a juror tells a party or the judge that improper pressure was used in the jury room, or that something contrary to law was done during deliberation. Then the judge may recall the jury to investigate the matter.

A juror who violated the law during a trial or deliberation can be subject to fines and imprisonment. The taking of bribes, talking to people about the case, doing independent investigation, and bringing in other evidence are all improper. They can be cause for punishment of a juror and overturning of the jury's decision.

Losing parties in large cases will almost always investigate the jury in an effort to discover improper behavior. Since major trials are extremely expensive to hold, the risk of not getting a decision which will be confirmed on appeal is serious. For this reason many precautions are taken during all phases of the trial, including protecting the jurors from improper influence.

Throwing out the jury's verdict

After the jury's verdict has been given, either party

may ask the judge for a new trial if they believe the jury has decided the case on passion and prejudice rather than evidence. A judge has the power to grant the request for a new trial. Judges can also decide on their own that the jury ignored the evidence and declare a *mistrial.*

Either the judge or a later appeal court can also reduce the amount of money awarded by the jury if a jury is believed to have been swayed by passion rather than evidence. To avoid appeal after the verdict is in, judges may use this power to force an agreement between the parties. The jury's verdict is not the last word!

The rules regarding appeals are different for different courts. When the original judge refuses a new trial, an appeal court will grant one only if the judge made a significant legal error or there was no evidence to support the jury's verdict.

Problems with the adversary system

There are several problems with the adversary system as a method of finding truth and doing justice. One is that, just as in a trial by battle, the more effective fighters are likely to win, whether or not their cause is more just.

Another is that finding the truth may not be the best way of doing justice. The fact that people broke the law may not mean that justice requires their punishment, especially when laws are obsolete or appear unjust. Many civil rights cases in the 1960s in the United States involved people breaking unjust laws—such as the one requiring blacks to sit in the back of city buses.

When people are justified in breaking the law, the jury determines their guilt. Then it remains for the judge to decide how their justifications for law-breaking affect their punishment.

Another problem of the jury system is that the people making up the jury are not necessarily able to understand a given case, no matter how well presented. Once a case reaches a certain level of complexity, untrained people are unable to absorb what is being presented. Even if they can absorb it, they may be unable to sort it out in a useful way.

There is a movement today to eliminate jury trials in such complex cases because the logistics are so difficult. The group of cases known as the "asbestos cases" are an example of this impossible complexity. These cases involved hundreds of parties. A courtroom was set up in a large auditorium with tables for the hundreds of lawyers.

Yet another problem is the difficulty of presenting a jury case so flawlessly that a higher court does not overturn the initial decision. An appeal often turns on the question of whether or not evidence was properly presented to the jury, not whether or not the right result seems to have been reached.

CHAPTER 3

Alternatives to the Legal System

So far we have looked at the legal system in general and at juries in particular. Before developing a theology of jury duty, it may be helpful to also look at alternatives that have been proposed or are already in use.

It is interesting to note that the methods we now call "alternatives" were the ways in which all disputes were handled before the development of the modern legal system. In terms of human history the legal system is a newcomer.

We should also note that the number of disputes which reach the court system is small compared to the number of disputes resolved in other ways.

Think back over your last week. How many disputes did you have? Most were probably so minor you hesitate to call them disputes. Others may have required more serious attention. Disputes are the inevitable result of all human interaction. The fact that so few reach the courts may give us clues about ways to resolve even more of them without the courts.

Alternative Dispute Resolution Methods

Arbitration versus mediation

Alternative methods divide into two general categories: first, methods which preserve the adversary system, usually referred to as *arbitration*. Second, methods which replace the adversary system, usually referred to as *mediation*.

What is arbitration?

Arbitration may be thought of as a private mini-trial. Instead of going to court the parties agree to use arbitration. An agreement to arbitrate disputes is sometimes included in contracts.

An arbitrator or several arbitrators are chosen by the parties. If they cannot agree on one person it is common for each to choose one arbitrator and these two arbitrators to choose the third. The parties can decide whether or not to use lawyers in presenting their case.

The arbitrator may or may not have legal training. Usually, however, people are chosen as arbitrators because they do have legal training or are familiar with the issues involved in the dispute.

How arbitration works

In arbitration, parties present their cases to the arbitrator much as they would in a trial. Sometimes cases are presented by mail instead of in a meeting. After presentation of a case the arbitrator decides how to resolve the dispute. Sometimes the parties have agreed in advance that the decision of the arbitrator is final. Other parties prefer to reserve the right to take the matter to court if they disagree with the arbitrator's decision.

Arbitration has the obvious appeal of being much less complicated, and therefore both faster and less expensive, than a trial. There are as many variations of this method as people doing it. One attractive feature of private arbitration is that the parties can agree to do it any way they want. Even more attractive is the fact that what they do is their own business instead of a public spectacle. This can be important if there are trade secrets involved, or other reasons to keep the matter private.

Many courts have also begun to use arbitration to lighten their case-load. Legislation has been passed which allows these courts to order certain types of cases to arbitration. Court arbitration involves more set rules but is still much less complicated than a trial.

While there are other dispute resolution methods which preserve the adversary system, they tend to be variations on the theme of arbitration. That theme is the use of a private arbitrator instead of a judge, with each side giving its view of the case to the arbitrator who decides the case. When more than one arbitrator is used, arbitration begins to look more like a judgeless jury trial. Usually, however, a mutually agreed upon arbitrator controls the case in much the same way a judge controls a trial.

Arbitration is provided for in many contracts, and there are organizations that provide arbitrators. The largest organization is the American Arbitration Association. It has lists of approved arbitrators and rules for arbitration.

Christian Conciliation Service also offers arbitration in some areas. Arbitration has been growing as courts have become busier and the law more complex, resulting in slower and more expensive trials. In Los Angeles, it can take up to five years for a case to get to the courtroom.

What is mediation?

At first glance mediation looks much like arbitration. It involves the parties in dispute and a mediator. But there the resemblance ends. Mediation assumes that the best solution to the dispute is one which the parties themselves discover and agree on.

Mediation can only be voluntary since an unwilling participant would prevent the process from working. While in arbitration responsibility for resolving the dispute rests with the arbitrator, in mediation that responsibility stays with the disputing parties.

How mediation works

Mediation is hard work. Far from being a quick and easy way to resolve a problem, it is a method for restoring broken relationships. It means dealing with the present problems as well as deciding how the parties will relate to each other in the future.

The role of the mediator is to create an atmosphere in which the parties can be open with each other. This will hopefully allow them to work cooperatively and creatively toward meeting everyone's needs as the key disagreements and misunderstandings are addressed.

Some efforts have been made to combine mediation and arbitration into one process, notably by the Christian Conciliation Service. My experience is that the openness needed for a successful mediation is not possible when the mediator can opt to become an arbitrator. The adversary system requires guardedness, and mediation requires openness. I recommend trying mediation first. If this fails, the matter can be handed to an arbitrator who was not involved in the mediation. A proper mediation contract will prevent the use of evidence obtained in the mediation in any later arbitration or trial.

Diversion

There is a great variety of programs designed to keep people, especially juveniles, out of the criminal justice system. Diversion programs for both adults and children "divert" people from the system. For instance, first-time offenders may attend educational classes aimed at helping them change their behavior instead of marking them with a criminal record.

Drug and alcohol programs work to help people stop abusing these substances instead of jailing them for things they did while under the influence of drugs and alcohol. Usually the successful completion of a diversion program allows a person to make a new start with a clean record.

Victim Offender Reconciliation Program

Victim Offender Reconciliation Program (VORP) seeks to bring victims and the people who harmed them together. The aim is to work out a plan of repayment to the victim for any financial loss and to work at reconciliation between the people involved.

The program sees crime as the breaking of relationships and believes that by bringing people together the relationship can be healed. Offenders are helped to take responsibility for the harm they have done. This allows victims to understand the offenders' behavior. Both parties then work on a plan to pay back what has been lost (restitution) and make future intentions clear.

This VORP approach applies even when the victim and offender have never known each other. In such cases, the broken relationship is the human trust relationship which is basic to all human society. When injustices are acknowledged, equity is restored, and future intentions are made clear, it is possible to have genuine reconciliation.

VORP works before and after the court process

VORP is used for both convicted criminals and people diverted from the criminal justice system. A VORP meeting looks more like mediation than arbitration. The difference is that participation may not be entirely voluntary. The offender may be required to either participate in the VORP process or proceed through the regular criminal justice system. While ideally participation in both the VORP process and the resulting agreement is voluntary, it looks less voluntary than mediation when the court is involved in imposing the choice to use VORP.

A new variation on the VORP theme is in process. It involves convicted and sentenced prisoners who want to reconcile with their victims. In the prison at Vacaville, California, for instance, an inmate group called Victim Offender Reconciliation Group works to sensitize inmates to the damage their crimes have caused. It helps them take responsibility for what they have done, giving opportunities for symbolic restitution to the community where it is not possible to meet with the offender's actual victim.

VORP does not replace the legal system

VORP as currently practiced is not usually an alternative to the legal system itself, since offenders are referred or sentenced to it by courts. Because of its focus on direct negotiation and accountability, VORP nevertheless embodies alternative values and methods which seek to restore relationships rather than simply punish offenders. It does remove many cases from the court system. VORP, when well done, can be a beautiful incarnation of the gospel message.

Restorative Versus Retributive Justice

The court system is based on retributive justice

The legal system as we have described it is based on retributive justice. Society seeks to punish, to exact retribution from one who has violated its laws. If you rob a bank you go to jail. This does not return the money to the bank. Rather, it exacts a price from the robber which does not benefit the victim other than by satisfying the victim's desire for revenge.

There have been efforts over the years to rehabilitate offenders by offering job training as well as school classes in prison. However, rapidly rising prison populations make these efforts increasingly less effective.

There is much debate about the merit of putting people in prison. It is expensive. And there is evidence that prison tends to make people worse rather than qualify them for a productive future.

Many voices call for giving more attention to some root causes of street crime: unemployment, broken families, discrimination, and the quiet violence of ghetto-living which saps the human spirit of hope for the future. When life in prison is no worse—and in some ways better—than life outside, jail is no solution to the problem of crime.

When people are alienated from society to begin with, separation from society by imprisonment is no punishment and no incentive to change. The only benefit of prison then is to temporarily keep the individuals from committing another crime.

Restorative justice is a biblical alternative

Another approach to crime is "restorative justice." This model is based on the biblical principle of *shalom*, that wholeness which comes when there is righteousness, justice, and right relationships in the community.

In this model, criminal and even civil disputes are seen as broken relationships that affect the total society. The goal of restorative justice is the healing of this social wound and the restoration of the community's wholeness. Both VORP and mediation are based on this restorative justice model. Because it maintains distance and brokenness between people, the adversary system is contrary to this model.

The model of forgiveness on which restorative justice is based says that forgiveness can happen when there is the mutual recognition that (1) injustices have been recognized, (2) the equity between persons has been restored, and (3) future intentions toward one another are clear. When these things have been done, forgiveness can happen. (Ronald Claassen developed this peacemaking model as an extension of work done by David Augsburger.)

VORP is based on this model of forgiveness, as is any mediation. A simple VORP example is for me to tell you that I realize it was unjust for me to steal your television set, for me to pay you back for the set, and to tell you that I won't steal from you again. When those three things happen to your satisfaction, forgiveness is possible.

A restorative justice system would work at the root causes of broken relationships through social programs. It would use mediation in its various forms to deal with that brokenness. There would be no room for revenge in such a system. Neighborhood and city-wide dispute resolution centers would handle local disputes. Regional and national centers would handle disputes involving people from different areas.

This vision of dispute resolution centers is already being successfully implemented in many neighborhoods. However, it will take many years of concentrated effort for such models to replace the current legal system to any significant degree.

We need to continue to ask whether we, as Christians, should support the current legal system. Is it doing the best it can under the circumstances? Are we willing to work to replace it? To criticize without offering workable solutions is seldom helpful. What do we have to offer? What does the concept of restorative justice have to say to the current system?

CHAPTER 4
Theological Issues

Most people in both Canada and the United States accept jury service without questions. Most Christians have no theological or religious questions about it. The goal of this chapter is to examine the heritage which has led many Mennonites, and others who value Anabaptist beliefs, to reject all participation in government. It is to ask how they have come to reject even jury service, and to compare that position to the majority view in an effort to help readers define their own stance.

Anabaptist Roots

The Reformation begins

During the Middle Ages the Catholic Church was

the only church in all Europe. Religious diversity and toleration as we know it did not exist. All children were baptized and became members of the church soon after birth. People were either members of the true church or heretics.

A movement to reform the church was begun in the sixteenth century by reformers such as Martin Luther. That movement, now called the Reformation, spread throughout Europe.

One reformer who made a significant impact was Ulrich Zwingli, a preacher hired by the city-state of Zurich in what is now Switzerland. Because of his relationship to the state, he was reluctant to move as quickly as some of the disciples who gathered around him. Agreeing with Luther that the church must be universal, he continued to require the baptism of children.

Anabaptists break away from the state church

Zwingli's position on baptism resulted in conflict with some of his disciples. Finally in 1525 three of them broke with their teacher. They did so by baptizing each other on confession of faith in Jesus Christ as they understood it from the Bible.

They believed that the church must be a completely voluntary body of adult believers, separate from the state. They totally rejected infant baptism. Adult baptism was the sign of membership in this new, voluntary church. Because of this they became known as the Anabaptists, the re-baptizers.

In 1525 the Anabaptists separated themselves from the institutional church of Zurich. By that act they also separated themselves from participation in the government that authorized the operations of the state church.

Until then, being a citizen of a state meant being a member of the church it approved and sponsored. The church likewise approved and supported the acts of the state. When the first Anabaptist was baptized on confession of faith in open defiance of this church and state union, he broke the law.

Anabaptists in conflict with the government

Many early Anabaptists died as martyrs because their understanding of God's will for them and their desire to follow Christ in life led them into conflict with the government. Why did Anabaptists believe so differently from other people of their time? Why did their spiritual successors have difficulty with jury service? In an effort to find answers, we will examine the Anabaptist understanding of the relationship between the church and the state.

How Anabaptists studied the Bible

The Anabaptist refusal to obey the government in spite of great risk was rooted in their commitment to follow Jesus' life as closely as possible. This life of *discipleship* (a "disciple" is a person who follows after a teacher) was built on a foundation of both individual and group prayer and Bible study.

Any person could interpret the Bible, but personal understandings of the Scriptures were tested by the group of believers. The Anabaptists believed that the Holy Spirit would lead the group to truth. Obedience to God's will as discerned in this way was to be absolute. The basic Anabaptist Bible study principle was a commitment to obey as much as they could understand.

This obedience to God led Anabaptists to reject many practices sanctioned by the church. They refused the use of deadly force, participation in government courts, the holding of government offices, and the swearing of oaths.

Our task here will be to study these Anabaptist understandings of the way to discipleship and see how they speak to us. We will also ask whether later Mennonite interpretations of these issues help us in our decision-making on the issue of jury service today.

In discussing "the Anabaptists" we need to recognize that the movement was broad and diverse. The Swiss Brethren who first pulled away from Zwingli established the line of understanding we will be discussing. It is that understanding which has most affected modern Mennonites. (For a larger discussion of the diversity of the Anabaptist movement see James Stayer's book *Anabaptists and the Sword*.)

The sword

"The sword" here represents the use of deadly force by governing authorities. It brings to mind the apostle Paul's words in Romans 13:4 that the one in authority does not "bear the sword in vain."

Anabaptists generally refused to bear the sword

Most Anabaptists understood the Bible as a whole, and the New Testament record of Jesus in particular, to teach that Christians were not to bear the sword. They were to reject deadly force. The way of Jesus was one of love, including love for enemies, so they could not accept the use of deadly force to resist evil.

Jesus' teaching in Matthew 5:38-39 was taken as a literal instruction not to resist a violent evil person: "You have heard that it was said, 'Eye for eye, and tooth for tooth.' But I tell you, Do not resist an evil person. If someone strikes you on the right cheek, turn the other also."

This understanding developed into the doctrine of *nonresistance*, which was and is the most common position of Mennonites and other historic peace churches to this day. (For a more thorough discussion of nonresistance as it is understood by Mennonites today see my book *The Anabaptists Are Back: Making Peace in a Dangerous World*, Herald Press, 1991.)

Using the sword involves judging someone

The use of the sword involves judgment of a person or group of people by another person or group. According to the Anabaptist view, only God can judge. The believer is not to judge other people's lives in relationship to God. Neither should the believer cut off other people's chance for redemption by killing them.

Nowhere in the New Testament does Jesus advocate the use of deadly force. His teachings are consistent with the Old Testament emphasis on love of neighbor and righteousness. Jesus lives out the Old Testament prophecy of a suffering servant Messiah who brings in a new covenant between God and humankind.

Jesus meant what he said about loving enemies

Jesus' teaching about love of enemies was not totally new. The Old Testament has much to say about the same theme. The apostle Paul quotes from Proverbs 25 when he tells his readers that, rather than take revenge, they should feed a hungry enemy (Rom. 12:19-20).

Jesus also added a new twist to the old teaching about love of the neighbor. In the story of the good Samaritan (Luke 10:30-37), Jesus extended the definition of neighbor from "fellow Israelite" to "all people."

Anabaptists were not eligible for government service

Historical evidence shows that early Christians shunned anything to do with the sword and the civil justice system. They were not even allowed to serve in these positions until A.D. 173. This situation was completely reversed in the fourth century. At that time, Constantine and the Roman Empire officially converted to Christianity and required that all soldiers be Christian.

Like the early Christians, the Anabaptists began as legal heretics. They were ineligible for public office and the military. Since the Anabaptists also included many of low social rank, their firm teaching against serving in the military or as law-enforcement officials was theoretical. Of course it was their teaching against military service, among other things, which made them heretics in the first place.

Mennonites were first given legal status in Holland in 1795. Some then began to hold public offices. By World War II Dutch Mennonites had held many legislative, administrative, and judicial offices. They had also participated in the military to a higher degree than Mennonites in any other country. The situation in Germany was similar.

Holding public office seemed to go hand in hand with giving up the doctrine of nonresistance. In Europe today Mennonites tend to see little conflict between their obligations to the church and to the state.

Summing up the Anabaptist view

The Anabaptist argument against the use of the sword may be summed up as follows: Jesus showed in his life and by the way he died that nonresistant love toward enemies is his way.

Jesus accepted the power of the government and honored it by submitting to it. He did not, however, accept the use of deadly force, or any type of violence, for himself or his followers. The only warfare Jesus approved of was spiritual warfare. Jesus asked us to follow him as disciples and live as he showed us. Jesus died for everyone. If we kill a person we kill someone for whom Christ died.

We are to see Christ in our enemies as much as in our friends. We are to overcome evil with good. Participating in the military means agreeing to kill. Participating in government service as a police officer, judge, or other official who makes or enforces the law is also a use of the sword. This is because the threat of deadly force is what empowers these offices.

Protestants and Catholics alike have disagreed with this Anabaptist understanding of the sword. As official state churches during the Reformation, both baptized all infants into the church and required church membership of all citizens. To be a universal church meant that all state functions were performed by church members. It also meant that all crime was committed by church members. All disputes were between church members. For all practical purposes, the justice system was also the system of church discipline.

It is easy to see how, in this setting, the biblical passages on church discipline and those on the believer's relationship to the state could result in views totally different from those of the Anabaptists. Judging others is not only acceptable but required when church discipline is the issue.

The free churches disagree

The Anabaptists were part of a larger Protestant "free church" movement. This movement gradually gained acceptance even by some rulers who in turn allowed their subjects a formerly unknown religious freedom of choice.

There was, however, no movement to rethink the understandings of the Christian's relationship to the state. Most free church members continued to regard military and judicial service as the fulfillment of an honorable Christian duty, just as they had as Catholics. Modern Baptist and other evangelical churches tend to follow this understanding.

There was no incentive to reject the historic bond between church and state in favor of one of the curious sects, such as the Mennonites, who taught and lived another way. The explosive growth enjoyed by the early Anabaptist movement during turbulent years of persecution waned quickly. Toleration quieted the witness of this radical people in a way that persecution had not.

Comparing Anabaptist and majority views

Our question today is whether either the Anabaptist *or* the Protestant/Catholic view of the relationship between church and state is helpful in determining what faithfulness requires of us as potential jurors.

We live in a different setting than the sixteenth-century world. Our laws are written by a democratically elected government and we enjoy freedom of religion, with some limitations. Lawlessness and violence are somewhat controlled by resorting to violence only rarely. Some police officers retire without ever having shot at anyone. Our military is voluntary and only infrequently engages in deadly action.

In this setting, is the Anabaptist understanding that believers should separate themselves from the military and law-enforcement positions valid?

The Anabaptist view is that the use of deadly force is always wrong for a Christian. This view is based on the belief that one cannot love people and kill them too. Since we are to love all people, just as Christ did, no office which requires the use of deadly force is appropriate. This view requires the examination of any official role to determine whether or not its function is based on the use of deadly force.

The Protestant/Catholic view, greatly simplified and called the "majority" view, is this: Government is ordained by God to protect the good and punish the evil. It is the duty of the Christian to work to those same ends. While the use of deadly force is regrettable, people may bring it on themselves by their stubborn disobedience to the law. Killing such people is justified and not a violation of the law of love.

The majority position regards official action as being of a different order than personal action. It holds that the private actions of Christians are to meet a higher standard of love and forgiveness than their actions on behalf of the government.

The Anabaptist view, on the contrary, holds that Christians are bound by the same law of love in *all* relationships. They must therefore refuse an office that violates this law of love.

These same conditions apply to military participation. For Anabaptists there is no way to participate in an organization devoted to the efficient killing of others. For the majority of Protestants and Catholics, however, it is reasonable to participate in the military as long as the military engages only in "just" wars.

The definition of a *just war* has always been a problem, however. Today many are convinced that a just war is impossible because of the huge numbers of civilian casualties that would result from bombing in general, and nuclear bombs in particular.

The majority position on jury service is that it is an orderly and desirable way to administer justice. Christians, because of their compassionate nature, are best qualified to perform it properly. While there is greater concern when the death penalty is involved, that concern has to do not with jury service itself but with the matter of condemning a person to death.

For the strict Anabaptist, on the other hand, the important question is whether or not jury service itself involves the use of the sword. The decision about personal participation is based on the answer to that question.

The court system and violence

Is jury service a form of violence? The state uses the legal system to control the actions of its members. People who violate the law can be called to account. Deadly force may be used at several stages in the process. Police may use deadly force in the capture of a lawbreaker or during an attempt to escape or harm an officer. Court orders may be enforced with deadly force. Control of people in prison seems possible only by the threat of deadly force.

Many people believe that the prison system itself is violent. Jurors are participants in the system that captures, tries, and punishes people. It then imprisons them in what is perhaps the most violent environment on earth. Are Christians participating in this system making them party to the threat of deadly force which allows the system to function? This is the question which must ultimately be answered by each prospective juror concerned about the Anabaptist understanding of Jesus' law of love.

Drawing the line on violence

Participation in the military may be used as an analogy to jury service. A juror does not hold a gun. Neither does an army cook or an air force jet mechanic. Yet all are necessary to the process by which their different systems operate. Estimates are that nine supporting troops are needed to keep one combat soldier in the field. Is the jet mechanic more responsible for the war effort than the cook? Is the munitions specialist who loads bombs and cannon shells more responsible than the mechanic? At what point do we draw the line on participation in violence?

When we do draw lines, they often appear arbitrary. Mennonites requesting military exemptions in World War I were sometimes asked why it was killing to work in an army hospital and not killing to grow wheat which fed the army. An Anabaptist would bring this question to jury service as well.

Holding public office

The early Anabaptists could find nothing in the New Testament to tell them how a Christian person was to perform a government office. And they felt government offices could note operate under God's law of love. Thus they determined that being a judge, police officer, or other law enforcer was outside the perfection of Christ. Such jobs should be filled by people whose first loyalty was not to the kingdom of God.

Because the majority position allowed its people to separate their public from their private lives, they never saw holding public office as a problem. Following the law established by a God-ordained government could not violate the law of love, although as private individuals people were to forgive rather than seek revenge.

Swearing oaths

> "Again, you have heard that it was said to the people long ago, 'Do not break your oath, but keep the oaths you have made to the Lord.' But I tell you, Do not swear at all: either by heaven, for it is God's throne; or by the earth, for it is his footstool; or by Jerusalem, for it is the city of the Great King. And do not swear by your head, for you cannot make even one hair white or black. Simply let your 'Yes' be 'Yes,' and your 'No,' 'No'; anything beyond this comes from the evil one" (Matt. 5:33-37).

Anabaptists accepted this passage from the Sermon on the Mount quite literally. They refused to swear any oath, either as required for legal business or in ordinary profanity. This remains the position of their modern-day successors, the Mennonites.

While God is portrayed in the Old Testament as swearing oaths to the patriarchs, God does not instruct people to swear oaths. Rather, the Old Testament use of oaths seems to have been more an accommodation to a hard-hearted people than a requirement.

This accommodation includes the regulation of false swearing. Leviticus 19:12 says, "Do not swear falsely by my name and so profane the name of your God. I am the Lord." This admonition coupled with Jesus' specific command to avoid oaths is the reason why Mennonites generally still refuse to swear a legal oath.

Today courts and other government departments accommodate this reluctance to swear by allowing people to *affirm*. Many courts have altered their standard oaths to read something like this. "Do you solemnly swear or affirm that the testimony you give here today is the truth and nothing but the truth?" However, when the avoidance of swearing is achieved by changing the word to "affirm," one may well ask why it is done at all.

Avoiding the oath is one of the relatively few ways North American Mennonites have continued to separate themselves from the world. The choice not to swear is a problem only when encountered by an unaware and possibly flustered official. A gentle response may solve the problem and provide a helpful interchange.

This has been the case for me serving as a lawyer and as a notary public for many years. I was often asked to swear oaths. I would simply say something like, "I affirm the truth of what I say here." That was always enough. When I expected to be "sworn in," I would tell the clerk ahead of time that I was an affirmer. I had many interesting conversations about the Sermon on the Mount as a result.

In the Matthew 5 passage Jesus is likely talking about the swearing of an oath to confirm the truthfulness of a testimony or promise. Did Jesus mean for his teaching to apply to oaths as used by jurors and witnesses in modern courts?

The Task of Judging Others

What does the Bible say about judging?

The purpose of courts is to judge. But Christians generally, and those who value the Anabaptist view in particular, have felt that judging others is contrary to biblical teaching. The case is stated most clearly in Matthew 7:1-2: "Do not judge, or you too will be judged. For in the same way you judge others, you will be judged, and with the measure you use, it will be measured to you" (NIV).

When Jesus was asked in Luke 12:13 to tell one brother to divide an inheritance with the other, he refused, asking who had appointed him judge. In John 7:24 Jesus castigated the Pharisees for judging by appearances. In John 8:15 Jesus said that the Pharisees judge by human standards, whereas he judged no one. At the same time, it is interesting to note how often Jesus seemed to judge the Pharisees when he accused them of hypocrisy.

Paul also spoke of not judging, particularly in regard to issues such as the weaker believers objecting to eating meat sacrificed to idols. At the same time he allowed for church judgments in the area of discipline.

In his letter to the Corinthians, Paul, addressing a church member having his father's wife, says, "I have already passed judgment on the one who did this." But he then explains, "What business is it of mine to judge those outside the church? Are you not to judge those inside? God will judge those outside" (1 Cor. 5:3, 12, NIV). Paul clearly recognized that the discipline within the church is a proper form of judging while judging the behavior and motives of those outside is not.

Separation from worldly things

A theme repeated throughout the New Testament is the call for believers to maintain some distance from the cares of the world while still participating in the activities of daily life. Just as the Creator clothes the lilies of the field, so you also will be cared for. This detachment from the cares of life seems to carry over into the realm of passing judgment. This attitude was important to the Anabaptists.

When the Anabaptist leaders met at Schleitheim in 1527 to record their common confession, they were faced with the question of "whether a Christian shall pass sentence in disputes and strife about worldly matters, such as the unbelievers have with one another." They responded by saying that they should do as Christ did and refuse. They saw this not as an abdication of civic responsibility but as a positive witness to their attempt to follow Christ in life.

Is this kind of separation from the world viable for us today? People who oppose jury service are often asked whether they would want all morally upright people to refuse to be on the jury if they were defendants. It is not helpful to say that can't happen, because it can. What do we make of Jesus' refusal to judge between the two brothers?

Perhaps it is helpful to see Jesus' admonition in Matthew 7 in its larger context. The command not to judge is followed by a further command not to try to remove a speck from your brother or sister's eye until you have removed the plank from your own. This expansion of the flat prohibition of judging may indicate that judging is acceptable when your own life is in order. Is Jesus being ironic? Or is he saying that those who guard carefully against self-righteousness may make right judgments?

Summing up the Anabaptist view

Anabaptist theology, as we have seen, raises a number of questions about jury service. Does jury service involve us too closely with the coercive power of government? Should we be making judgments which have some impact on others' lives—especially when the result can be destructive? Can we make the oath or affirmation required for those preparing to serve?

But these questions are balanced by other questions. Is it realistic or right to try to "keep our hands clean"? Do people with a vision of biblical justice have a responsibility to bring that vision to bear on the realities of our world? If so, is jury service a proper way to do that?

Complex matters are involved. The next chapter will try to lead you through these issues by asking a series of questions. The personal stories in the appendix illustrate how several people have wrestled with the issue in their own lives.

CHAPTER 5

The Decision-making Process

The purpose of this chapter is to help guide you through the main issues discussed thus far. Regardless of your initial stance on jury service, the goal now is to guide you toward your own informed decision.

You may begin the process with Section A below. If you answer "yes" to a question, move to the next question. If at any point you answer "no," move to Section B for a discussion of how to be exempted from jury service. Whatever your decision, discuss the matter with your group of believers. Plan to obey as much as you can understand of God's will for you.

Working Through the Issues

- On the most basic level, is it proper for Christians to be involved in any government activities?

- If you decide that you, as a Christian, can participate in government to some extent, are you willing to participate in the court system?
- Would your participation in the court system include jury service under any circumstances?
- Would your willingness to serve on a jury extend to civil cases? (If so, what limitations would you place on your participation regarding subject matter, parties involved, degree of jury involvement, and range of possible verdicts?)
- Does your willingness to serve on a jury under some circumstances extend to criminal cases? (If so, what limitations would you place on your participation regarding the nature of the crime, the accused person, the role of the jury, and the possible sentences?)

When You Cannot Serve

Some people accept service on any jury; others oppose all service. Still others stand between these positions—their willingness to serve depends on the particular case. This section is for persons sometimes or always opposed to service.

There are several basic ways to avoid jury service:

- Inform the court of your claim to an automatic exemption under one of the court's categories.
- Be exempt under one of the categories that requires the court to make a decision in your case. This can include religious objection or financial hardship. Such an exemption will be granted after the judge is satisfied that you qualify.

- Be excused "for cause" during jury selection. If you are not excused before jury selection begins, you will be able to renew your objection or make it for the first time during jury selection.
  If you feel you cannot make a fair and impartial decision in the particular case, or if the length of the case or your personal circumstances impose a hardship, you will have an opportunity to say so. If your reason is rejected initially by the court, you may still be excused at a lawyer's request, since lawyers do not want unwilling jurors.
- Be excused on a peremptory challenge. This exemption may be granted without explanation. Jurors who have made it clear that they are being forced to serve against their will are likely to be excused in this way by one of the lawyers.
- Refuse to serve. This is against the law. It can be punished by jail sentence or fine, depending on the court. Courts are strict about jury service since they depend on jurors and cannot afford to let people think service is optional. There is no legal conscientious objector status for jurors.

Alternative Service for Jurors

Many people who object to military service are motivated by such sincere religious conviction that they would go to prison rather than serve. This has been demonstrated many times and many governments have seen fit, in the face of such conviction, to allow people an alternative form of useful employment.

The impact of alternative service is similar to military service in that both require the removal of people from their communities and careers. Alternative service is often designed to be unattractive so people will not choose it simply because it is easy.

Conscientious objector status is a legal option today in part because Mennonites and other groups organized in opposition to military service. Opposition to jury service has been much less organized. This was true in the past because people like Mennonites were not called to serve as long as they remained outside of the mainstream of society.

Even today there is no great demand for organized opposition because unwillingness to serve involves little personal risk. To save time, judges will excuse people they know to be firmly opposed to jury service on religious grounds. The confessions of some Mennonite groups include firm statements of opposition to jury service. Members of these groups are usually exempted from service without difficulty when the judge is shown the group's statement. (Sample confessions are reproduced in Appendix C.)

Perhaps it is time to consider the creation of an alternative form of service for those religiously opposed to jury service. The spread of alternative dispute resolution systems does remove some pressure from the courts. Perhaps this pressure could be further alleviated if people opposed to jury service served in some way with an alternative dispute resolution center.

This could increase the number of cases these alternative programs could handle and at the same time increase public awareness of these alternatives. Nonjurors who performed such peacemaker service could refuse jury service with greater integrity than those who simply refused to participate in the system.

It would be possible to implement this alternative service without creating another bureaucracy. A court could simply assign, as one of its automatic exemptions, a certain number of hours of voluntary service with an alternative dispute resolution service. Individuals could then make their own arrangements. Making this alternative service available to its members would also encourage the church itself to become more active in dispute resolution.

Conclusion

Many Mennonites today are being asked to serve on juries. They are answering the call in a variety of ways. Some are responding without question. Some are simply refusing to serve. Many are in between, wrestling with questions of when and how to serve.

Some church groups and conferences are addressing the issue. A number have adopted positions. Ask your church conference whether the issue has been explored in recent years.

The personal experiences of people who have been called can be helpful. Several are included in the appendix of this book. You may also want to talk to others in your congregation and community who have been called.

The issues and answers are complex. Dialogue is important. Share your questions and experiences.

APPENDIX A
Personal Stories

Howard Zehr: Pennsylvania

Some time ago I received a long letter from the judges of the county where I live. It informed me that I had been selected for possible jury service. This was my court system, it explained, and thus it was my privilege and duty to serve.

That had never happened to me before. I suppose I have always been viewed as a somewhat marginal person. As a student, later as a professor at a black college in the South, still more recently as a relative newcomer to this community, my name never seemed to come up. Now, apparently, I was "in."

It was not that I have ignored the question of jury service. I had sat in many courtrooms, had assisted defense attorneys in selecting juries, and had worked with offenders whose fates were in the hands of juries. For the past eight years, in fact, courts and sentences had been the primary focus of my work. So I was acquainted with how juries operate. I had often contemplated what my response would be if I were called. But the question remained hypothetical.

Now it was up to me. The questionnaire I received from the judges asked a crucial question: "Do you have any religious or other reservations about sitting in judgment on another person? Yes or no?"

As a Christian, how could I simply answer "no"? But if I marked "yes," I would be unlikely to serve. Moreover, my answer might seem hypocritical since I have sat and do sit in judgment of others in my capacities as teacher, employer, and the like. And I knew that this question was only the beginning. I would be questioned further during the jury selection process.

Given my concerns about and experiences in criminal justice, I knew it was improbable that I would actually end up on a jury. The prosecutor would undoubtedly eliminate me. But the question remained one that I had to answer.

I looked to the church for guidance. After all, here is a key intersection between church and state, one of the areas of ordinary life where questions of the Christian's participation in political activities are most likely to arise. I assumed that a peace church, where such issues are so vital, would have a great deal to say on the subject.

I asked someone to do a preliminary search through historical church records. She found surprisingly little.

The issue was touched on from time to time, often in conjunction with discussions of voting, litigation, and the swearing of oaths. Many of the statements she found indicated that Mennonites should not serve or should avoid service if possible.

Rarely were elaborate reasons given. Those mentioned seemed to focus on the believer's responsibility, in the words of one statement, to be "subject to but . . . not part of the civil administration power" and on the fact that judgments made by jurors were carried out by powers which bore "the sword."

Often, however, statements on political participation were silent on the subject of juries. Some allowed for participation but prohibited it in death penalty cases.

A more comprehensive recent statement came from the Peace and Social Concerns Commission of the Lancaster Conference (one of the clusters of congregations into which the Mennonite Church is divided) in 1980. This statement notes that some Mennonites have found service to be a good experience. It says that trial by one's peers is a reasonable way to insure justice and that judgments by jury provide an arena where Christians can help correct injustices.

It concludes that jury duty may be part of "responsible Christian citizenship." It encourages Mennonite participation with three qualifications.

First, people should face the responsibility of service with the prayerful backing of God's community.

Second, support should be given to those whose convictions differ.

Third, no one should participate when the death penalty is involved.

One thing, at least, is clear. An increasing number of Mennonites are being called to jury service. Some are responding without question. Others are doing so hesitantly, seeking guidance. It is the responsibility of the church to respond.

I did not find existing statements to be fully satisfying. The following, though, are questions and considerations that seemed relevant to me.

It is important to distinguish between civil and criminal juries. In criminal cases, focus is on establishing blame and imposing pain. The state brings charges against an individual and the result will involve an assessment of blameworthiness and punishment.

In civil cases, however, the dispute is between two parties, with the judge and jury acting as arbiter. Focus is on a settlement more than guilt or punishment. I have little problem in principle with participation in civil trials. The critical questions are posed by criminal cases.

The distinction between capital and noncapital cases is also important. As the various church statements note, it is difficult to see how a follower of Christ could participate in a decision to take a life.

A number of arguments can be made for encouraging Christians to serve on juries. Jury service can be viewed as a civic duty, as one relatively "safe" way in which Christians can take responsibility in the political process. Moreover, Christians are called on to do justice, to see that the oppressed receive fair treatment. Jury service may be one way to put that into practice.

Perhaps, then, jury service is an opportunity to

bring Christian compassion and understanding to bear on individual lives. As one person put it recently, "If you or your children were on trial, what kind of juror would you want? Wouldn't thoughtful, caring, nonviolent Christians be your best hope?" If Christians all washed their hands of all this, justice might be left to those with less compassion.

But real cautions must be noted as well. I wonder sometimes about the extent to which God intends us to have power over other people's lives, especially when this is such highly coercive power. Is such power consistent with servanthood?

Moreover, I am constantly impressed with the injustice and illogic of "criminal justice." It is frequently arbitrary. It often discriminates. It callously ignores victims. It focuses on punishment rather than reformation. Perhaps most important, it is inherently violent and not simply because criminal law is enforced by "the sword."

The normal response to crime in our society is to imprison offenders. The result? The United States imprisons more people per capita than any other industrial nation except Russia and South Africa.

Prisons in this country are, by their very nature, tremendously violent settings. To sentence someone to prison is to sentence them to one of the most violent environments existing in this society. How can I participate in a decision that is not only enforced by threat of violence, but actually results in violence to the person sentenced?

Finally, I take issue with the way the jury's role has come to be restricted in our age. Earlier in American history, the jury was designed in part as a check on errors and abuses by government. Juries were to rule on matters of fact—is this person guilty, given the facts? But they also had the right and duty to rule on the law itself. If a law was felt to be unjust, juries had the power to nullify the verdict, to refuse to convict, or to speak out against the law in other ways.

As the power and scope of government has grown, discomfort with such citizen power has also grown. The scope of juries' authority has been systematically narrowed. Today jurors are instructed to find guilt or non-guilt on the basis of the facts of the case. They cannot comment effectively on the wisdom or justice of the law itself.

Nor are juries allowed to decide the remedy in individual cases. Juries rarely have a say in the actual sentence pronounced. Indeed, they may not even know what the possible sentence is. Instead, the jury focuses on one basic issue: is the person guilty as charged? The real issue—how can we solve the problems involved in this offense?—is obscured. Focus is on guilt rather than problem-solving.

With these issues still unresolved, I received my summons for actual jury duty some weeks later. I decided to participate rather than to seek to be excused, hoping that the process might help bring clarity. Since this was a lower court, cases and penalties would be relatively minor.

I was among the first set of people to be questioned in the *voir dire* or questioning process. Potential jurors were questioned by the judge, prosecutor, and defense attorney to determine their suitability and desirability on a jury.

An interesting dialogue developed during this questioning. It touched on issues of justice, attitudes toward offenders and the legal process, and the biblical perspective on judging. Information began to unfold about the case. A black man was charged with receiving two stolen bicycles. He was to be tried—in a totally white courtroom—under a law that took no notice of the value of the stolen property. The charge, and possibly the penalty, would be the same as for a serious car theft.

Initially I had been willing to sit on this jury, even with my reservations. During this discussion, however, I became increasingly bothered. If I were to help return a guilty verdict, I would be expected to put my faith in the judge's good judgment in passing sentence.

I as a juror would have nothing to say about the penalty or the law. I would be expected to make my decision on strictly legal grounds. I could not consider causes, the context of the offense, the offender's or victim's needs, or moral considerations.

I realized that I could not in good conscience return a guilty verdict in such a case. Thus I informed the court that I would not be able to do so and explained why. I was excused.

I am still undecided about jury service, although I can respect a variety of positions. One thing is now clear, though. The easiest response would be to avoid the issue by seeking an immediate exemption. But this seems irresponsible to me. Many citizens do that simply because they do not want to be bothered.

The experience and the dialogue are important,

both for ourselves and for the court. One can usually be exempted, as I was, along the way. But to opt out at the beginning, without some sort of dialogue or statement of principle, is not a course I can take.

Elsie M. Epp: Saskatchewan

What would you do if you received a registered letter which stated "You are commanded to attend Her Majesty's Court of Queen's Bench at the Court House [on a certain date] at the hour of 10 o'clock in the forenoon to serve as juror. . .?"

I had never given that question much thought. But when such a letter arrived at my house, I knew I had to find answers to a lot of questions—and quickly!

Normally in Saskatchewan, I would have received such a letter at least six weeks prior to the date on which I was to be at the Court House. But I received mine just eight days before. According to the sheriff this was because an extra panel of potential jurors was needed during June.

I began by calling on people involved in Justice Ministries with Mennonite Central Committee. I called a friend who recently completed peace studies at seminary. I talked to members of my small group and shared my dilemma with the church on Sunday morning. The counsel I received varied. But what a surprise to discover that no one I asked had any first-hand information or experience!

During the five days before I had to hand in my Juror Information Return, I concluded I would need to request relief from jury service on the basis of conflict with my personal religious beliefs.

I wrote a statement in which I tried to express those beliefs. I tried to make it clear that as a Christian I do want to be a citizen concerned about and involved in bringing about justice for all. However, it seems to me that the definition of justice and the way in which justice is achieved as defined by our legal system differs significantly from what the Bible teaches.

The biblical concept of justice is primarily concerned with restoring relationships between the offended and the offender. Seeking justice is made possible through an attitude of mercy and willingness to risk giving someone another chance.

By contrast, I see our legal system defining justice as a process whereby those accused of committing crimes receive a fair hearing according to the laws of the land. They then, if found guilty, receive their just punishment. The jury plays an important role in this process leading to punishment for the guilty. I could not in good conscience see myself becoming a part of such a dead-end process.

I went on to say that as a juror, I would need to have primary concern for the demands of the law and could give only secondary concern to the individuals involved, whether victims or offenders. I doubted I could merely judge a person as guilty or not guilty when many Scriptures admonish me not to judge.

I pointed out that the requirements of the laws of the land and of the laws of God might conflict in some other ways. If so, I would hope to have the courage to be loyal to God.

Finally, I expressed reservations about whether the present system does indeed make justice available to those who are poor and uneducated.

The sheriff indicated that the judge would consider releasing me from duty if I could (by the next day) get an official letter from the Mennonite church supporting my stance as official church policy.

Of course, I could not provide such a letter. To the best of my knowledge, we as a General Conference Mennonite Church have never made a statement about jury service.

The sheriff explained that my personal religious beliefs did not qualify me for an exemption. However, if I really felt strongly about my beliefs, I should speak up in court. Unfortunately, I did not ask how and when that might be possible.

Arriving at the courtroom, I soon realized that the court moves rapidly and routinely through the process of calling up, challenging, setting aside, and swearing in jurors. It became clear that there would be no opportunity for questions or statements unless I made such an opportunity. By the time my name was drawn from the box, they had already called about forty names and had selected eleven of the twelve jurors.

When my name was called, I simply stood up and said, "I believe this is the appropriate time to inform the court that my personal religious beliefs do not allow me to judge my fellow human beings in the way required of jurors."

At this point I received a lecture from the judge. He said it was a good thing there were not more people like me or our country would be in chaos. People like me did not deserve to have themselves and their families protected by the law. I was putting my personal beliefs ahead of my responsibility as a citizen.

He reminded me that personal religious beliefs did not qualify me for an exemption. I replied that I knew that. However, I wanted it understood that I would not be able to support a guilty verdict if required to sit on the jury.

After consulting with the three defense lawyers and the lawyer for the Crown, the judge said he could require me to defend my position. However, he didn't think there was much point, and since it had already taken so long to select a jury, he would excuse me. On my way out, he emphasized I was not to give the impression to others that it would be easy to get out of jury service.

As a result of this experience, I am profoundly impressed with the strength and boldness available to us through the prayer support of fellow believers. I am greatly encouraged to know that when we find ourselves in a dilemma, we have many resource people within the church from whom to draw on for information and support.

I am surprised that, as a Mennonite church, we have done so little studying of this issue. I hope that will change.

I am concerned that personal religious beliefs count for so little in our society. I suppose I've known that, but until now I had never faced it directly. I fear that others who may decide to take a similar position may find the judge not ready to excuse them.

I know that not everyone in our church family would come to the conclusion I did. There are many related questions and implications which I have not yet considered. I only hope that my struggles may encourage all of us to search more diligently for God's word to us in this area of "living in but not of the world."

Ron Meyer: Ohio

In the fall of 1977 I received a summons for a term of jury service to begin October 6, 1977. The summons was from the U.S. District Court in Columbus, Ohio. I assume my name was obtained from a voter registration list.

I had to fill out and return some form. I was especially interested in the form in which one can claim exemptions from jury duty. I can't remember all the categories of people excused but some stand out. Doctors, teachers, and, I believe, lawyers were exempted. Farmers and factory workers were not. The "excused" categories were mostly professions.

I remember thinking that most of the jurors must be blue-collar workers and housewives. Experience proved this assumption fairly accurate.

I searched my conscience to see if I had serious objections to serving on a jury. I didn't want to do it. I spent several days thinking about the whole thing.

In the end my conscience kept me from making up an excuse or trying to get out of it in a devious way. I felt I honestly had no reasons based on faith in God or moral principles that would prevent my serving.

In addition, I realized that if I were ever on trial (it could conceivably happen because of our refusal to pay some taxes) I would want to be given a fair hearing. I would want a jury that listened to me and acted in good conscience. I felt I could offer honesty and fair-mindedness as a juror. This is what I would expect if I were on trial.

So I returned everything requested and prepared for the first big day.

I anxiously dialed the collect long-distance number the evening of October 5. I was surprised and happy to hear that my jury need not report the next day. The case had been settled out of court.

As of this writing I've been summoned fifteen times. I've had to make the trip four times. I've served a total of twelve days of jury duty and have been in two trials.

The swearing-in is a real experience. All fifty of us potential jurors are to raise our right hands and say "I do" to the preliminary oath before court officials start asking questions and excusing jurors. There are so many people and it's confusing, so I don't make a ruckus then. I stand up like everyone else but do nothing.

It's different if I'm selected as a juror. All those selected are to swear to tell the truth or be honest or something like that. I've always refused to do that. Each time either the clerk (who administers the oath) or the judge realizes that I want to affirm, rather than swear, before I can say much. The clerk has trouble remembering the way that goes so he stumbles through it. I say "yes" and sit down.

Most people in the court don't realize what is going on but some do. I think it's a fairly significant witness, especially with the judge I've had. He is a gruff, demanding old gentleman. Everyone is afraid of him. So to interrupt him or someone in his court causes a little stir.

Concerning the oath itself—its wording, its spirit, and its basic assumptions all bother me. The more I hear it the more I'm repulsed. The use of the name of God as part of a "holy" ritual to make someone tell the truth disturbs me. Jesus' command to simply say "yes" or "no" seems so simple, open, and sensible.

There are other bothersome things. Judges wield much power. They can determine how a trial will go by admitting or not admitting evidence, by sustaining or overruling objections. I'm disturbed that a person is given so much power and is assumed to be able to use it fairly. This is particularly a problem since federal judges are political appointees.

The seven defendants I've encountered have all been black. Nearly all my fellow jurors have been white, rural, and in my judgment, tending toward racism. This raises serious questions about fairness.

In addition, the real "thinkers" of our society are mostly excused from jury service. I don't feel good about drawing juries from groups of people who have not had enough power to obtain blanket exemptions. It's not fair.

There is nothing holy about twelve people making a decision. The decision could be wrong, but our system treats it as sacred. And despite the judge's repeated urgings, some jurors make their decisions with the crowd, ignoring misgiving to avoid standing out.

I was surprised—but one of the hardest things I've done was answer "Yes" when the jury was polled after its verdict was read in my first trial. "Yes," I agreed: the verdict was my verdict. I helped decide that these persons were guilty. But what if they weren't? Either way, they would go to prison. I feel bad about helping to put someone into the prison system.

In America we revere the "law" and the court system. It provides "justice," we say. But it is full of inequities. It is not fair; it is not just.

Maybe it is the best we can do. But it doesn't deserve our allegiance, our top loyalty. Our allegiance belongs to God.

My experience in court makes me more glad to be a Christian. I believe in a God who is just, who is right, whom I can trust, who is utterly dependable. If I had to look to the law or the court system as the ultimate truth and authority, I would be lost—because that system fails.

The experience has made me realize more strongly that I don't belong to any kingdom of this world. I belong to Christ's kingdom. In that sense the experience has brought me new freedom and peace.

Would I do it again? I'm not sure. I would have to consider it carefully and share it with friends.

My Own Jury Story

As I was working on this book, I received a jury questionnaire from my county Jury Commissioner. Since California has eliminated nearly all exemptions from jury duty, this questionnaire was designed to obtain personal information for the use of attorneys during jury selection, not to find out whether or not I would sit on a jury. I filled out the form, noting that as a Mennonite pastor who was an active member of the State Bar, my presence on a jury panel would waste the courts' time.

Shortly after the final manuscript was in the publisher's hands, I received a notice to report for jury service the following Monday. The notice said: "You are obligated to serve as a trial juror in the courts of Fresno County since you have been duly selected, qualified, and summoned at this time." It also had a number to call "Should you have any questions as to your ability or qualification to serve as a trial juror at this time or feel that you should be excused or your service deferred to a later date." It then listed several California statutes protecting employees from employer retaliation.

My wife laughed, and suggested that I'd better read the book I'd written. I knew from other people's experience that you could easily get deferred to a later time over the phone, but that to be excused you had to appear in court in person. If I believed that I could not serve under any circumstances, I should certainly call in and ask to be excused. That should also have been noted on my questionnaire. Since I don't have a blanket objection to all jury service, I would have to go see whether the particular case was one I could participate in. We planned to be out of town on Monday, so I called in and was excused until Thursday.

Thursday came. I was nervous. There were already 200 people in the jury assembly room when I arrived, and no one was in charge. There was a sign asking us to place our payroll cards in the basket and be seated. I did.

The afternoon before the United States and its allies had begun bombing Iraq, and there was a television tuned to CNN which most people watched with rapt attention. I tried to read, but the noise and general commotion was too much. A clerk came in a while later and called the roll, then sent three groups of jurors to courtrooms. I was not sent.

We waited a while longer, then the clerk came back and said we were excused until 2:00 p.m. That was fine with me, since I had some work to do. I went to the law library in the courthouse, passing through the metal detectors, and spent some time working.

At 2:00 my group was back, waiting.

Two men behind me were talking. One said, "I can't believe I'm here, they just assume you're willing to do this. I don't believe in this system at all. I don't see how I can judge someone."

That made me realize we had not been given any information about our task. We had not been given a pep talk. We had simply been told to come and go.

At 2:30 we had roll call again, then were excused for the day. The clerk said, "The case you were waiting for was settled, partly because you were here waiting for them. Call our recording after 4:30 next Wednesday for instructions."

Our county requires jurors to be on call for two weeks, and this call-in system saves a lot of trips to the courthouse. It is quite efficient. Thinking about what the clerk said, I realized she was right. The pressure of knowing that jurors are waiting to hear the case is a great incentive to settlement. "Settle right now, or take your chances."

I called again on Wednesday and was told by the recording to call again at 11:30 a.m. Thursday. I called then and was told to call at 4:30. At 4:30 I was told to report at 9:00 a.m. Friday, the last day of my service. I had filled it with appointments, having expected to be finished with jury service. So much for that great idea.

Friday morning found about 200 of us waiting again. Again there was a roll call and a group of jurors was sent out. Again I waited and waited. Around 11:00 we were told to come back at 2:00. This time I had no work I could do without going home, but the drive and lunch would take most of the time.

I went for a walk, had lunch, and kept reading my book. I went to the law library and looked at the latest issues of *Jury Verdicts Weekly* which gives a synopsis of the interesting jury verdicts entered in California. I discovered that knee operations like I had last year generate a lot of malpractice cases, and that Fresno juries are still conservative compared to their counterparts in Los Angeles and San Francisco.

Back to the jury assembly room for roll call. I was tired by now. Sitting is hard work. Then the fifty of us were all sent to a courtroom. I knew it well. It is the basement courtroom where alimony and child support payments are handled, and other cases when those are done.

We were all alert now. The courtroom was empty except for a bailiff and a young black man. Was he the defendant we were going to be asked to judge? Nothing happened. We just waited. An hour later the judge came in with a rueful expression. "I want to tell you why you are waiting here," he said.

As it turns out, we were evicted from the jury assembly room so that it could be used for a swearing in ceremony for new judges. The case we were to hear wasn't going to proceed, since the person charged with shoplifting had not bothered to show up. That meant, however, that the sixteenth and last case set for trial that day was ours. It was scheduled for five to six days, and was for a violation of the leash law. We were all stunned at the thought of sitting in that courtroom for a week to decide about a leash law violation. But not to worry, the judge told us, he had talked the defendant into continuing the case for two weeks so his attorney could start a murder trial on Monday. Our service was ended. We were excused.

I spent a lot of energy worrying about how to respond to different situations that might come up during my jury service, and none of them did. What had worried me most was the swearing-in, which would happen suddenly and with no chance to alert the clerk that I don't swear oaths. When in courtrooms before, I had been one of the people controlling the action. Being part of the furniture with others in control was not a good feeling.

So I'm still puzzled. Was this leash law case one I could hear in good conscience? How about the shoplifting case? I would need to know more about each to know whether they were appropriate for me. I do feel let down at having spent so much time waiting for nothing, but I also know that the system requires jurors to wait so that people will be moved to resolve their own disputes. As strange as it is, I do feel a certain sense of having done my civic duty. If I can do that by sitting and reading a book, why not? Next time I'll bring spare batteries for my radio.

APPENDIX B
Leader's Guide

This booklet is intended for use by individuals or groups concerned about jury service. The leader's guide will be most helpful when used in a group setting. It is designed to cover the material in four to six sessions, though extra sessions would allow more time for the use of outside resource people and materials.

Suggested Resources

Be sure to obtain your own denominational, conference, or other appropriate doctrinal or confessional material on jury service and the Christian's relationship to the state. Many groups do have such statements. Also contact your denominational offices to discover resource people and materials that relate to the subject. See the end of this book for a list of selected resources.

Personal stories are compelling tools in any discussion. You may want to refer to the stories contained in Appendix A. You may also want to invite local people—lawyers, judges, and others who have done jury service—to share their perspectives on the workings of juries. For suggestions about lawyers, contact your local or area bar association.

Jury selection is a public procedure. You could arrange to visit a courtroom during that process. Check with the court's clerk about schedules for this.

Suggested Procedure

First meeting

Pass out books. Introduce the subject and reasons for discussing it. Present proposed study outline, including outside materials. Modify that outline as determined by the group. Ask group members to share briefly their own experiences with jury service to acquaint each other with shared experience. If time allows, invite members to share concerns about the issue. Ask the group to read Chapter 1 for next session.

Second meeting

Imagine yourselves as a group without a legal system. One of your members accuses another of robbing him or her. How do you deal with this? Determine both what happened and what to do about it. Come up with as many different methods as possible, listing them on a board or pad.

Were any of these methods like the ones described

in Chapter 1? How were they different? Which method is better? What is good or bad about the methods in Chapter 1? Encourage the group to imagine freely and creatively. Ask them to read Chapter 2.

Third meeting

Invite a judge or a lawyer to describe his or her views of the legal system in general or to talk about the adversary system, trial work, and jury selection. Since it is impossible to cover all that is relevant, help your speaker in identifying points to be covered and allow some time for interaction with the group. You might want to follow up this session without the speaker at the next meeting.

If you do not have an outside speaker, you might have group members who have gone through the jury selection describe their experiences and let the group respond to their stories.

At the appropriate point, discuss the jury selection process as described by the speakers or Chapter 2. How does the process feel to you? How might it be improved? Is any part of the jury selection process a contradiction of Christian values? Ask the group to read Chapter 3.

Fourth meeting

Begin the discussion of the decision-making process of a jury with input from a speaker or a summary of the Chapter 3 material. How do you feel about the process? Is any of it contrary to a Christian viewpoint? How do the alternatives discussed in Chapter 3 compare to the jury system? Are there other alternatives that could improve on the system?

Draw on the personal experience of any of your members or have a speaker on one or more of the alternatives. Ask the group to read Chapter 4.

Fifth meeting

Begin with a brief summary of Chapter 4 by leader or resource person. You may want additional input on viewpoints inadequately covered in the chapter, particularly in regard to your denomination's official position.

Discuss violence and deadly force. Does the group feel that the legal system in general, or the jury system in particular, is violent? Is jury service really analogous to military service? Are oaths a problem for your group? Find out what oaths are used in your local courts. Conclude with issues your group found most interesting in the theology discussion. Ask the group to read the personal stories in Appendix A.

Sixth meeting

Work through Chapter 5 together, discussing those issues important to your group. Identify problematic areas and determine if the group wants to pursue them further. Some people may be ready to make a final decision on the issue now. Others will need more time to arrive at a position.This is a personal process that needs to proceed at its own pace.

The discussion of jury service may lead to interest in exploring other criminal justice issues. For a list of other resource materials, contact the Mennonite Central Committee offices listed at the end of this book.

APPENDIX C

Sample Confessional Statements

Most confessional statements of Mennonites and related groups do not specifically mention jury service. Each one has sections on nonresistance and relationship to secular government which assume that the believer has no role in government or in opposing enemies by force.

Nearly all confessions make explicit the duty of the believer to obey and pray for the governing authorities, except when the government demands action which violates God's law. Oaths are specifically forbidden in nearly all confessions.

Since Mennonites and related groups did not receive calls to jury service in significant numbers until the last few years, it is not surprising to find little in confessions and statements of doctrine on the subject.

Mennonite Church Confession of Faith—1963

Article 18. Love and Nonresistance

We believe that it is the will of God for his children to follow Christian love in all human relationships. Such a life of love excludes retaliation and revenge. God pours his love into the hearts of Christians so that they desire the welfare of all men. The supreme example of nonresistance is the Lord Jesus himself. The teaching of Jesus not to resist him who is evil requires the renunciation by his disciples of all violence in human relations. Only love must be shown to all men. We believe that this applies to every area of life: to personal injustice, to situations in which people commonly resort to litigation, to industrial strife, and to international tensions and wars. As nonresistant Christians we cannot serve in any office which employs the use of force. Nor can we participate in military service, or in military training, or in the voluntary financial support of war. But we must aggressively, at the risk of life itself, do whatever we can for the alleviation of human distress and suffering.

Article 19. The Christian and the State

We believe that the state is ordained of God to maintain law and order. We seek to obey the New Testament commands to render honor to the authorities, to pay our taxes, to obey all laws which do not conflict with the higher law of God, and to pray for our rulers. The church should also witness to the authorities of God's redeeming love in Christ, and of his sovereignty over all men. In law enforcement the state does not and cannot operate on the nonresistant principles of Christ's Kingdom. Therefore, nonresistant Christians cannot undertake any service in the state or in society which would violate the principles of love and holiness as taught by Christ and his inspired apostles (Scottdale, Pa.: Herald Press, 1963, pp. 23-24).

(There is no relevant content change in this confession from the 1632 Dordrecht Confession.)

Church of God in Christ, Mennonite—1938

8. We believe that Christians, true followers of Christ, should not engage in waging war, nor in serving an office in the magistracy; nor that they should even sit as jurors to pass judgment upon offenders of the law, to have that enforced by civil power, which bears the sword; nor that they should vote for those civil magistrates, who are to exercise power, which power is of no force without the sword, or the fear of it, or some other bodily punishment, for we hold that by voting we vote the power that is enforced by the sword, which is contrary to the non-resistant doctrine. This doctrine has been confessed by the Waldenses and Mennonites, as may be seen in their confessions. (John Holdeman, *A History of the Church of God*, p. 161, in Urbane Peachey, ed., *Mennonite Statements on Peace and Social Concerns.)*

Amish Christian Church

. . . seeing neither Christ nor his apostles prescribed to believers any laws or rules according to which they should govern the world; therefore, we do not take any part in political affairs in any form, such as voting for officers, serving as officers of any position. We do not prosecute nor go to law in any way, nor do we take part, or serve in war in any form, even if it is called non-combatant. (Reprinted in John Howard Loewen, *One Lord, One Church, One Hope and One God: Mennonite Confessions of Faith*, Elkhart, Ind.: Institute of Mennonite Studies, 1985, pp. 212-213.)

General Conference Mennonite Church—Unruh/Alexanderwohl Statement of Faith

. . . We believe that according to the teachings of Jesus Christ and the apostles, and the example of our lord and master and the first Christians, believers cannot take part in any carnal strife or warfare, either domestic, religious, or civil, or between individuals, factions or nations. The believer is admonished to have peace with all men, to love his enemies and pray for them. (Reprinted in Loewen, p. 154.)

Bibliography

The books and articles listed here are offered as helpful resources for further study. Some are topical; others are general. Some annotations are offered to mark those of particular interest. Mennonite churches and educational institutions are likely to have many of these works available.

Augsburger, Myron. *Pilgrim Aflame*. Scottdale, Pa.: Herald Press, 1967.

A fine historical novel based on the life of Michael Sattler, one of the first Anabaptists.

Barrett, Lois. *The Way God Fights*. Scottdale: Herald Press, 1987.

Berkhof, Hendrik. *Christ and the Powers*. Translated by John H. Yoder, Scottdale: Herald Press, 1962.

Cadoux, C. John. *The Early Christian Attitude to War*. New York, N.Y.: The Seabury Press, 1982.

Invaluable for understanding the change in the church from its beginnings to today.

Claassen, Ron; Zehr, Howard; and Ruth-Heffelbower, Duane *VORP Organizing: A Foundation in the Church*. Elkhart, Ind: Mennonite Central Committee US, 1989.

Dyck, Cornelius J., ed. *An Introduction to Mennonite History*. Scottdale: Herald Press, Second Edition, 1981.

Estep, William R. *The Anabaptist Story*. Grand Rapids, Mich.: William B. Eerdmans Publishing Co., 1973.

Friedmann, Robert. *The Theology of Anabaptism*. Scottdale: Herald Press, 1973.

General Conference Mennonite Church. *A Christian Declaration on the Way of Peace*. Newton, Kan.

Harnack, Adolf. *Militia Christi*. Trans. David McInnes Gracie. Philadelphia, Pa.: Fortress Press, 1981.

Heffelbower, Duane. "The Christian and Civil Disobedience," *Direction*, vol. 15, no. 1 (Spring, 1986), 23-30.

Discusses how to deal with the situation where obedience to God and to the state conflict.

Kaufman, Donald D. *What Belongs to Caesar?* Scottdale: Herald Press, 1969.

A standard work on this difficult question.

Kehler, Larry. *The Rule of the Lamb, a Study Guide on Civil Responsibility*. The Christian and Civil Responsibility. Newton, Kan.: Faith and Life Press, 1978.

Keim, Albert N., and Stoltzfus, Grant M. *The Politics of Conscience*. Scottdale: Herald Press, 1988.

Shows how Mennonites used the political process to gain conscientious objector status.

Klaassen, Walter, ed. *Anabaptism in Outline*. Scottdale: Herald Press, 1981.

Anabaptist source materials.

Klaassen, Walter. *Mennonites and War Taxes*. Newton, Kan.: Faith and Life Press, 1978.

Paying taxes for war purposes raises questions relevant to jury service.

____________. *Anabaptism: Neither Catholic nor Protestant.* Waterloo, Ont.: Conrad Press, 1973.

Klassen, William. *Covenant and Community. The Life, Writings and Hermeneutics of Pilgram Marpeck.* Grand Rapids: Eerdmans, 1968.

The writings of one of the first Anabaptists.

____________. *Love of Enemies, The Way to Peace.* Philadelphia: Fortress Press, 1984.

Kraybill, Donald B. *The Upside-Down Kingdom.* Scottdale: Herald Press, Revised Edition, 1990.

Becoming a classic work on separation from the world as a Christian ethic.

Lapp, John A., ed. *Peacemakers in a Broken World.* Scottdale: Herald Press, 1969.

Loewen, Howard John. *One Lord, One Church, One Hope, One God: Mennonite Confessions of Faith in North America. An Introduction.* Text Reader Series. Elkhart, Ind.: Institute of Mennonite Studies, 1985.

National Service Board for Religious Objectors. *Statements of Religious Bodies on the Conscientious Objector.* Washington, D.C.: National Service Board for Religious Objectors, 1951.

Military service and jury service have many issues in common.

Ruth, John L. *Conrad Grebel, Son of Zurich.* Scottdale: Herald Press, 1975.

Historical novel about one of the first Anabaptists. A readable and helpful resource for understanding the beginnings of the radical reformation.

Sider, Ronald J. *Christ and Violence.* Scottdale: Herald Press, 1979.

Sider, Ronald J., ed. *Cry Justice!* Downers Grove, Ill.: Inter-Varsity Press, 1980.
Examines biblical texts on justice issues.

Swartley, Willard M. *Slavery, Sabbath, War, and Women.* Scottdale: Herald Press, 1983.
One of the most helpful books on how to read the Bible and apply it to current issues. The section on war is relevant to issues surrounding jury service.

Umbreit, Mark. *Crime and Reconciliation.* Nashville, Tenn.: Abingdon Press, 1985.
Examines creative options for handling victims and offenders from a biblical justice angle.

van Braght, Thieleman J. *The Bloody Theater or Martyrs Mirror of the Defenseless Christians.* Trans. Joseph F. Sohm. Scottdale: Herald Press, 1975.

van Ness, Daniel W. *Crime and Its Victims: What We Can Do.* Downers Grove: InterVarsity Press, 1986.
A good examination of biblical and contemporary justice.

Wenger, J. C. *Pacifism and Biblical Nonresistance.* Focal Pamphlet No.15. Scottdale: Herald Press, 1968.

Yoder, John Howard. *The Christian Witness to the State.* Institute of Mennonite Studies Series Number 3. Newton, Kan.: Faith and Life Press, 1964.

___________. *The Original Revolution.* Scottdale: Herald Press, 1971.

___________. *The Politics of Jesus.* Grand Rapids: William B. Eerdmans Publishing Company, 1972.

Zehr, Howard, and Jackson, Dave. *The Christian as Victim.* Akron, Pa.: Mennonite Central Committee, 1981
Examines the experience of victimization and discusses how Christians can respond when victimized.

Zehr, Howard. *Changing Lenses: A New Focus for Crime and Justice.* Scottdale: Herald Press, 1990.

The single best resource on restorative justice.

____________. *Mediating the Victim-Offender Conflict: The Victim Offender Reconciliation Program.* Akron, Pa.: Mennonite Central Committee, 1980.

Provides overview of the VORP process and rationale. Includes case study by Earl Sears.

____________. *Retributive Justice, Restorative Justice. New Perspectives on Crime and Justice.* Occasional Papers No. 4. Akron, Pa.: Mennonite Central Committee, 1985.

A comparison of the two models or visions of justice.

____________. *Who Is My Neighbor? Learning to Care for Victims of Crime.* Akron, Pa.: Mennonite Central Committee, 1985.

Describes experiences of victimization and gives direction on how individuals/church can best respond to victims. (Companion slide set available.)

Audiovisual Resources

Crime: The Broken Community. A 12-minute slide set by Mennonite Central Committee.

Looks at criminal justice process from the point of view of the victim, the offender, the judge, and the Bible. Stresses need for alternatives allowing for restitution and repair. Also available in VHS videotape.

Crime: Mediating the Conflict. An 11-minute slide set by Mennonite Central Committee.

Focuses on the Victim Offender Reconciliation Program through a case study.

The Forgotten Neighbor. A 10-minute slide set by Mennonite Central Committee.

Dramatization of the impact crime has on the victim. Designed to help churches and other groups recognize victimization as a crisis experience. Can be used with the booklet, *Who Is My Neighbor*?

Additional Resources

For additional information, contact the following:

MCC U.S. Office of Criminal Justice
21 S. 12th Street
Akron, PA 17501
Phone: 717 859-3889

Victim Offender Ministries Program
Box 2038
Clearbrook, BC V2T 3T8
Phone: 604 850-6639

The Author

After eleven years of law practice, Duane Ruth-Heffelbower closed his law office to enter seminary. He is, with his wife, Clare Ann, a founding copastor of Peace Community Church—Mennonite, of Clovis, California, where he and Clare Ann continue to serve.

Duane has experience in criminal and civil jury trials, as well as military court-martials. He is a professional mediator. He was involved in the creation of the Fresno, California, Victim Offender Reconciliation Program, and works with it as a mediator. He is also a volunteer chaplain for the local police department.

Through his involvement with justice issues in law practice, the military, and community-based justice programs, Duane brings a unique perspective to the Christian's participation in the jury system.

Growing up in Newton, Kansas, Duane was heavily involved in church life. After marrying Clare Ann, he became involved in General Conference Mennonite Church work, serving on the General Board, Division of Administration and Spiritual Emphasis Committee.

Duane and Clare Ann are part time Evangelism and Church Development staff for Pacific District Conference (General Conference Mennonite Church).

Duane holds a B.A. from Kansas State University; a J.D. (doctor of jurisprudence) from Golden Gate University, San Francisco, California; and an M.Div. from Mennonite Biblical Seminary, Elkhart, Indiana. He is the author of *The Anabaptists Are Back* (Herald Press, 1991).

Duane and Clare Ann have a son, Andrew.

PEACE AND JUSTICE SERIES

This series of books sets forth briefly and simply some important emphases of the Bible regarding war and peace and how to deal with conflict and injustice. The authors write from within the Anabaptist tradition. This includes viewing the Scriptures as a whole as the believing community discerns God's Word through the guidance of the Spirit.

Some of the titles reflect biblical, theological, or historical content. Other titles in the series show how these principles and insights are practical in daily life.

1. *The Way God Fights* by Lois Barrett
2. *How Christians Made Peace with War* by John Driver
3. *They Loved Their Enemies* by Marian Hostetler
4. *The Good News of Justice* by Hugo Zorrilla
5. *Freedom for the Captives* by José Gallardo
6. *When Kingdoms Clash* by Calvin E. Shenk
7. *Doing What Is Right* by Lois Barrett
8. *Making War and Making Peace* by Dennis Byler
9. *A Life for a Life?* by Vernon W. Redekop
10. *Helping Resolve Conflict* by I. M. Friedmann
11. *Jesus' Clear Call to Justice* by Dorothy Yoder Nyce
12. *To Bless All Peoples* by Gerald Schlabach
13. *Questions That Refuse to Go Away* by Marian C. Franz

The books in this series are published in North America by:

Herald Press
616 Walnut Avenue
Scottdale, PA 15683
USA

Herald Press
490 Dutton Drive
Waterloo, ON N2L 6H7
CANADA

For overseas distribution or permission to translate, write to the Scottdale address listed.